I0760142

THEODORE ROOSEVELT

PIVOTAL PRESIDENTS

PROFILES IN LEADERSHIP

THEODORE ROOSEVELT

Edited by Randy Shattuck

Published in 2018 by Britannica Educational Publishing (a trademark of Encyclopædia Britannica, Inc.) in association with The Rosen Publishing Group, Inc.
29 East 21st Street, New York, NY 10010

Distributed exclusively by Rosen Publishing.
To see additional Britannica Educational Publishing titles, go to rosenpublishing.com.

First Edition

Britannica Educational Publishing
J.E. Luebering: Executive Director, Core Editorial
Andrea R. Field: Managing Editor, Compton's by Britannica

Rosen Publishing
Kathy Kuhtz Campbell: Senior Editor
Nelson Sá: Art Director
Brian Garvey: Series Designer
Alison Hird: Book Layout
Cindy Reiman: Photography Manager
Bruce Donnola: Photo Researcher
Supplementary material by Randy Shattuck

Library of Congress Cataloging-in-Publication Data

Names: Shattuck, Randy, editor.
Title: Theodore Roosevelt / edited by Randy Shattuck.
Description: First edition. | New York: Britannica Educational Publishing in Association with Rosen Educational Services, 2018. | Series: Pivotal presidents: profiles in leadership | Includes bibliographical references and index.
Identifiers: LCCN 2016001001 | ISBN 9781680486315 (library bound)
Subjects: LCSH: Roosevelt, Theodore, 1858–1919. | Presidents—United States—Biography. | United States—Politics and government—1901–1909.
Classification: LCC E757 .T379 2016 | DDC 973.91/1092—dc23
LC record available at http://lccn.loc.gov/2016001001

Manufactured in China

Photo credits: Cover, p. 3 (portrait), Stock Montage/Archive Photos/Getty Images; cover, p. 3 (background), pp. 22, 36 MPI/Archive Photos/Getty Images; cover, pp. 1, 3 (flag) © iStockphoto.com/spxChrome; p. 6 Bob Thomas/Popperfoto/Getty Images; pp. 8, 16, 21, 33, 42, 46, 57, 59 Encyclopædia Britannica, Inc.; p. 13 National Park Service; p. 14 © AA World Travel Library/Alamy Stock Photo; p. 18 Brady-Handy Collection/Library of Congress, Washington, D.C.; p. 26 FPG/Archive Photos/Getty Images; p. 29 Library of Congress, Washington, D.C.; p. 30 National Archives, Washington, D.C.; pp. 38-39 Buyenlarge/Archive Photos/Getty Images; pp. 40, 61 Library of Congress Prints and Photographs Division; p. 45 © Everett Collection Historical/Alamy Stock Photo; p. 47 Library of Congress, Washington, D.C. (LC-DIG-stereo-1s02353); p. 49 File:Alaska_boundary_dispute.jpg. Adapted by Rudyologist from Historical Atlas by William Shepard (Henry Holt and Company, 1923) in the collection of the University of Texas Libraries, The University of Texas at Austin (PD); p. 51 © Photos.com/Thinkstock; p. 65 Annie Griffiths Belt; interior pages flag Fedorov Oleksiy/Shutterstock.com

Table of Contents

Introduction

Theodore Roosevelt came into office as the twenty-sixth president of the United States just before his forty-third birthday. He offered Americans the Square Deal and was called the Trust Buster.

Theodore Roosevelt was the youngest president of the United States. He had been vice president under William McKinley, who was assassinated by an anarchist in 1901. Roosevelt took office as the twenty-sixth president just before his forty-third birthday. He was elected in his own right in 1904.

Theodore Roosevelt had tremendous energy and high spirits. He was not only a statesman but also a cowboy, naturalist, hunter, explorer, and soldier. No guest was more welcome at the White House than an old friend from the days when he worked on his North Dakota cattle ranch. A cowpuncher once appeared just before lunch when another friend, British ambassador James Bryce, was also to be a guest. Roosevelt said to him solemnly, "Remember, Jim, that if you shot at the feet of the British ambassador to make him dance, it would be likely to cause international complications." Jim replied with horror, "Why Colonel, I shouldn't think of it, I shouldn't think of it."

He advised everyone to lead "the strenuous life." While he was in the White House he rode horseback, played tennis, or took a rough cross-country walk daily. The

Roosevelt as a young man is pictured here wearing ranch clothing. He always admired frontier living.

companions on these exercises were known as the "tennis cabinet." In his autobiography Roosevelt wrote that often they would make a "point to point" walk, not turning aside for anything. If their route took them through Rock Creek Park in Washington, they might have to swim Rock Creek and scale the steep walls of cliffs. They swam the creek in their clothes when ice was floating thick in it.

Roosevelt brought the same vigor and determination to his presidency. He worked for peaceful relations between businesses and laborers through a program he called the Square Deal. He also tirelessly battled groups of big companies, called trusts, that tried to put smaller companies out of business, and he became known as a Trust Buster. He also asked Congress to pass legislation against the sale of contaminated food and drugs. In addition, Roosevelt wanted to preserve the country's natural resources. He set aside lands as national forests, which then became off-limits to companies looking for lumber, minerals, and water. Congress established the Forest Service in 1905 to oversee and protect the national forests.

Roosevelt also steered the nation toward an active role in world politics, particularly in Europe and Asia. One of his boldest acts came in 1903, when he helped Panama gain independence from Colombia and in exchange demanded a piece of land that cut through Panama. Roosevelt thus secured the route for construction of the Panama Canal, a vital waterway that connects the Atlantic and Pacific oceans. Furthermore, Roosevelt expanded the Monroe Doctrine. In 1823 President James Monroe had said that Europe should not become involved in the Americas. In 1904 Roosevelt added that the United States would police the countries of Latin America to make sure they fulfilled their agreements with other countries.

After leaving office in 1909, Roosevelt traveled to Africa on a hunting safari and then toured Europe. In 1912 he founded the Progressive Party, nicknamed the Bull Moose Party, and ran for president as its candidate. Both he and Republican president William Howard Taft lost to the Democratic candidate, Woodrow Wilson. During World War I Roosevelt was both a fierce advocate of the Allied cause and an outspoken critic of Wilson. The Republicans seemed ready to nominate him again for president in 1920, but he died in 1919.

After his death a New York police captain remarked, "It was not only that he was a great man, but, oh, there was such fun in being led by him." A New York newspaper publisher, James Gordon Bennett Jr., said of him, "While he is in the neighborhood the public can no more look the other way than the small boy can turn his head away from a circus parade followed by a steam calliope."

Chapter 1

Early Life, Education, and Marriage

In his autobiography Theodore Roosevelt tells us that his grandfather on his father's side was of almost pure Dutch blood. About 1644 his ancestor, Klaes Martensen van Roosevelt, came to New Amsterdam. "From that time for the next seven generations ... every one of us was born on Manhattan Island." The forebears of his father's mother came to Pennsylvania with William Penn. His mother came from Georgia, where her Scottish and English ancestors had settled before the American Revolution.

A Sickly Childhood

Roosevelt was born in New York City on October 27, 1858. His family lived in a luxurious home in a fashionable part of the city, for the Roosevelts were wealthy and had a secure social position. His father, Theodore Roosevelt Sr., was a noted businessman and philanthropist. His mother, Martha Bulloch, came from a wealthy, slave-owning plantation family.

He had a sister, Anna, about four years older than he and a younger brother and sister, Elliott and Corinne. Teedie, as he was called in his childhood, Ellie, and Conie were the closest of friends. "We Three" are often mentioned in the diaries he kept as a child.

Teedie had weak eyesight, and he suffered from asthma almost from birth. Many a night he sat propped up in bed, gasping for breath. Sometimes his father bundled him in blankets and took him for a ride in the carriage through the dark, silent streets, hoping that the gentle night breeze would give the child relief.

This portrait of Theodore Roosevelt Sr., Teedie's father, was taken around 1875. He was called Great Heart because of his kindness and generosity.

Theodore Roosevelt Birthplace National Historic Site

This is the birthplace of Theodore Roosevelt at 28 East Twentieth Street in New York City, as it looks today.

Theodore Roosevelt was born at 28 East Twentieth Street in New York City. Located near Union Square Park, the brownstone was home to the Roosevelts until 1873, when the family moved uptown to 6 West Fifty-seventh Street. The Twentieth Street house was torn down in 1916.

After Roosevelt's death in 1919, the Women's Roosevelt Memorial Association bought the property and built a reconstruction of the original home. Roosevelt's wife and sisters decorated the home with furnishings and objects from the 1860s, about half of which came from the original home. The National Park Service acquired the house in 1965 and made it a national historic site, which means that it has special protection. It contains five fully furnished period rooms, two museum galleries, and a bookstore. The collections housed at the site include some of Roosevelt's manuscripts, published books and articles, photographs, and letters and journals. There are also collections of campaign buttons, hunting rifles, and taxidermy specimens.

The Young Naturalist

He never went to public school. For a time his aunt Anna taught him, and he had private tutors. He became interested in natural history when he was a small boy, although he was so nearsighted that he could study only the things he "ran against or stumbled over." One day he observed a dead seal in a fish market. With a folding pocket ruler he made measurements of the seal and recorded them in a notebook. He finally acquired the seal's skull and with two of his cousins started the "Roosevelt Museum of Natural History." Their collections of bones, stones, dead mice, birds, frogs, and other items were kept in a dresser drawer. A maid once threw out a litter of mice. He was most hurt, as he wrote in his diary, by "the loss to Science! oh, the loss to Science!"

One day he and a cousin were returning home from a collecting trip. Their pockets were full, and each boy was carrying a toad on top of his head under his hat. Unfortunately they met a family friend on the street. Good manners forced them to tip their hats, and away went the toads.

Teedie was a sickly child and was taught by private tutors. He enjoyed studying natural science.

Just before he was eleven years old the family made a trip to Europe. In his diary of November 22, 1869, he wrote, "In the evening Mama showed me the portrait of Edith Carow and her face stirred up in me homesickness and longings for the past which will come again never alack never." Edith Carow was a friend of his sister Conie. Years later she became his wife.

On their return from Europe his father built a gymnasium in their home and urged the boy to build up his sickly body. In 1871, at the age of thirteen, however, he had a humiliating experience. On a trip that he made alone to a Maine lake two boys bullied him. Unable to fight back, he resolved to take boxing lessons and learn to defend himself. He was later a member of the Harvard University boxing team.

Though physically weak during his youth, Roosevelt developed a rugged physique the older he became by exercising persistently, and he became a lifelong advocate of strenuous physical and mental activity. He was a born competitor against both nature and his fellow human, and he used the same enormous energy throughout his public life.

Edith Kermit Carow, pictured here as an adult, was a dear childhood friend of Conie, Teedie's younger sister. Many years later Theodore and Edith married.

A Second Trip Abroad

A second overseas trip in 1872 was more successful than the first. The family made a voyage up the Nile River in a sailboat, and Teedie had a wonderful time collecting birds, learning their Latin names, and preparing their skins. He became quite skilled in both hunting and taxidermy.

The children, with two of their cousins, were lodged for a time with a family in Dresden, Germany. They formed the Dresden Literary American Club and read their creative writings to one another. One of the cousins wrote an essay describing Teedie: "You knew he was a naturalist on a small scale, he was a very amusing boy but he had a great fault he was very absent minded ... and then he always thought he could do things better than any one else."

He was fifteen years old when the family returned home. His health was greatly improved, and he began to tutor for his entrance into Harvard University. He began to be called by his first name instead of his nickname and never used "Teddy." He preferred to be called Theodore.

HARVARD UNIVERSITY

Roosevelt was a student at Harvard from 1876 to 1880. He was elected to Phi Beta Kappa, a leading academic honor society and the oldest Greek-letter society in the United States. While attending Harvard he studied an array of subjects, including natural history, zoology, forensics, German, and composition. He also enjoyed boxing and wrestling.

Roosevelt was not exactly a typical Harvard student. His energy and exuberance made him stand out from his more subdued classmates on the generally conservative campus. His rooms were packed with specimens and mounted animals. Professors found his incessant questions during lectures a challenge.

Roosevelt's father died of stomach cancer in 1878, leaving Theodore grief-stricken. After his father's death, Roosevelt decided to major in history and government at Harvard, fields that he believed would provide a good foundation for a career in public service. In June 1880 Roosevelt received a bachelor of arts degree, ranking twenty-first in his class.

Theodore Roosevelt studied history and government at Harvard College. He graduated in 1880.

Alice Hathaway Lee married Roosevelt on October 27, 1880, which was Theodore's twenty-second birthday. The Roosevelts were very active in New York City's social world and vacationed in Europe for five months in 1881.

Alice and New York City

In his senior year in college Roosevelt fell in love with Alice Hathaway Lee. She was from a well-known New England family of bankers. Alice and Theodore married in October 1880 and went to live in New York City.

Roosevelt attended Columbia Law School but spent most of the year writing his first book, *The Naval War of 1812*, which was published in 1882. The book closely examined naval combat during the war between the United States and Great Britain. It later became required reading at the US Naval Academy in Annapolis. Roosevelt disliked law school and left Columbia in 1882.

CHAPTER 2

State and National Politics

In 1881, when he was only twenty-three years old, Roosevelt ran for public office and was elected as a Republican to the New York State Assembly. In spite of his youth he made himself respected, and he quickly became known for his opposition to corrupt, party-machine politics. He was easily the leader of the Republicans in the legislature. He was reelected twice, and in 1884 he was chairman of the New York State delegation to the Republican National Convention.

DUAL TRAGEDIES

In early 1884 tragedy struck. On February 14 Roosevelt's wife died from kidney disease, just two days after the birth of their first child, Alice. Earlier the same night, in the same house, Roosevelt's mother had died from typhoid fever.

Roosevelt completed his term in the legislature and then went to his ranch in the badlands of Dakota Territory, in what is now North Dakota, to grieve and throw himself into cattle ranching. His sister Anna took care of the baby. He spent two years roping, riding, and spending time in the wilderness. During this time he became increasingly concerned about environmental damage to the West and its wildlife.

Roosevelt attempted to reenter public life upon his return to New York in 1886. He ran for mayor of New York City, but his bid was unsuccessful.

A Second Marriage

In December 1886 Roosevelt married his childhood playmate, Edith Carow, in London and settled down to a new life at Sagamore Hill, their newly built estate at Oyster Bay on Long Island. Between 1887 and 1897 they had five children—Theodore Jr., Kermit, Ethel, Archibald, and Quentin. The children were later called the "Roosevelt Gang" when they lived in the White House.

Roosevelt was a devoted father. He entertained his children and their many cousins and friends with the same energy he brought to everything else he did. Sagamore Hill was a happy place for children. There were picnics and overnight camping trips, swimming and rowing in Long Island Sound. There were wonderful Christmas and Fourth of July celebrations. He was not always in favor with the mothers. He let the children go swimming with their clothes on, and he took them on hikes from which they returned dirty and ragged. He was never too busy to have breakfast with the children or for a story before they went to bed.

The Roosevelts are seen here in the mid-1890s (*from left to right*): Theodore; Archibald (called Archie); Theodore Jr. (called Ted); Alice; Kermit; Roosevelt's second wife, Edith; and Ethel. Edith and Theodore had one more child, Quentin, who was born in 1897.

Edith Roosevelt

Edith Kermit Carow was born on August 6, 1861, in Norwich, Connecticut. She and Theodore Roosevelt grew up near one another in New York City, and Edith was especially close to Roosevelt's younger sister, Corinne, with whom she began attending a school for girls in 1871.

Although Edith and Roosevelt developed a romantic relationship as teenagers, he married Alice Hathaway Lee in 1880. Edith attended the wedding as a family friend. When Alice died, the distraught widower fled to his ranch in the Dakota Territory. On one of his trips to New York, he and Edith accidentally met, and their romance resumed. They wed on December 2, 1886.

During her years at the White House (1901–09), Edith Roosevelt made her mark in several ways. To create more living space for her large family, she and the president arranged for the construction of a new West Wing to house the presidential offices, which until then had shared the second floor with the family living quarters. With the help of an architectural firm, Edith also redesigned the interior of the mansion to enlarge the State Dining Room, and all the formal rooms were redecorated in elegant, classically simple lines and colors. The new style marked a big change from the ornate, dark velvets and fringes of the late 19th century.

Edith changed the job of First Lady in other ways. Even before moving into the White House, she had hired a social secretary to help with official mail. After her husband became president the secretary's job expanded to include communicating with the press, issuing official information on the family as Edith directed, and serving as a conduit for news about official functions. Another of Edith's innovations, a regular meeting with the wives of cabinet members to discuss moral standards and the appropriate level of spending on parties, struck some people as intrusive.

The Roosevelt children were a lively group that loved pranks. Edith was known for her patience and her ability to organize the household. Two family events were among the social highlights of the Roosevelt presidency: Alice's wedding and Ethel's debut.

After they left the White House in 1909, the Roosevelts traveled widely but retained their home at Sagamore Hill. Following her husband's death in 1919, Edith did more traveling, visiting Europe as well as South America, Africa, and Asia. Edith died at Sagamore Hill on September 30, 1948, and was buried in the family plot at the cemetery nearby.

THE RETURN TO POLITICS

Roosevelt began writing a history, *The Winning of the West*. But when President Benjamin Harrison offered him the position of civil service commissioner in 1889, he moved to Washington and for six years worked for civil service reform.

In 1895 he took the post of police commissioner in New York City. He tried to put an end to graft and corruption in the police force. He prowled the streets from midnight to dawn in a black cloak and a wide-brimmed hat pulled down over his face. Often his companion on these trips was Jacob Riis, social reformer and newspaper reporter, whose book *How the Other Half Lives* had awakened the public to the sufferings of the very poor. Roosevelt's efforts, however, were opposed by politicians and newspapers alike. He was vigorous and honest, but he did not always use good judgment or diplomacy.

Jacob Riis was a social reformer who shed light on the poor living conditions that lower-class people had to endure in New York City. As a police reporter for the *New York Tribune*, Riis became friends with Roosevelt, who was police commissioner at the time.

Roosevelt (*center*) led the Rough Riders, as the First Volunteer Cavalry was known, during the Spanish-American War of 1898.

The Spanish-American War

After two years Roosevelt resigned to accept President William McKinley's offer of a post as assistant secretary of the navy. McKinley sometimes thought his secretary was like a "bull in a china shop." He complained that "Roosevelt is always in such a state of mind."

At the time, war with Spain was brewing. Americans were angry over the brutal measures that Spain used to put down a rebellion against its rule in Cuba. Popular demand for US intervention grew even stronger after the unexplained sinking in February 1898 of the battleship *Maine*, which the United States had sent to Cuba to protect US citizens and property.

As war neared, Roosevelt, on his own authority, quietly ordered naval preparations. When war was declared in April 1898, he was commissioned a lieutenant colonel and raised the First United States Volunteer Cavalry Regiment. Roosevelt's friend Colonel Leonard Wood resigned as White House physician to command the regiment. Roosevelt, who resigned as assistant secretary of the navy, was second in command. The regiment was called the Rough Riders because it was made up of cowboys, miners, law-enforcement officials, and college athletes, among others. It was a flamboyant unit that received more publicity than any other unit in the war.

The Rough Riders were sent to fight in Cuba. Roosevelt famously led a daring charge up Kettle Hill (wrongly called the charge on San Juan Hill) during the Battle of Santiago. The battle made him the biggest national hero to come out of the war. When Wood was promoted, Roosevelt was made a colonel and given command of the regiment.

The Battle of Santiago

The battle that made Roosevelt a war hero was fought near Santiago de Cuba in June and July 1898. On May 19, 1898, a month after the outbreak of the Spanish-American War, a Spanish fleet under Admiral Pascual Cervera arrived in Santiago harbor on the southern coast of Cuba. US naval squadrons in the Atlantic Ocean, under Rear Admiral William T. Sampson and Commodore Winfield S. Schley, blockaded the harbor entrance.

To support the operation by land, US troops landed east of the city and penetrated its outer defenses. These troops included Roosevelt's Rough Riders, who joined in the capture of Kettle Hill and then charged across a valley to assist in the seizure of San Juan Ridge, the highest point of which is San Juan Hill. In an effort to escape capture, Admiral Cervera led his squadron out of the harbor on July 3. In the ensuing battle all the Spanish ships came under heavy fire from the US fleet and were beached in a burning or sinking condition. Two weeks later, Spain surrendered Santiago de Cuba. The US victory ended the war, suppressed all Spanish naval resistance in the New World, and enhanced the reputation of the US Navy.

A campaign image from 1900 depicts the Republican ticket of President William McKinley (*left*) and his vice presidential candidate, Theodore Roosevelt.

The War Hero Becomes Governor

On his return, the Republican bosses in New York tapped Roosevelt to run for governor, despite their doubts about his political loyalty. Elected in 1898, he became an energetic reformer, removing corrupt officials and enacting legislation to regulate corporations and the civil service. Those who were closest to him, however, notably Senator Thomas C. Platt, the Republican boss of New York, were disturbed by his gift for publicity and his startlingly unconventional approach to politics. Fearing him as a candidate for the presidency, they conspired to get rid of him and succeeded in putting him in the post with the most unpromising future (assuming that he would have a largely ceremonial role)—that of vice president of the United States when William McKinley was reelected in 1900. Roosevelt presided over the Senate for a week during a special session. But before the time for the regular session of the Senate, McKinley had been assassinated.

CHAPTER 3

The Presidency and the Bully Pulpit

Roosevelt's entrance into the presidency, like everything he did, was dramatic. He hastened to Buffalo, New York, where McKinley had been shot by a crazed anarchist. Assured that the president was recovering and out of danger, he joined his family at a camp in the Adirondack Mountains. With a few companions he climbed up Mount Tahawus. He was overtaken by a guide with the news that the president was dying. It was a 10-mile (16-kilometer) hike to the nearest road. Then followed a wild ride by horse and buggy for 40 miles (64 km) in the dead of night, over roads dangerously washed by heavy rains a few days earlier. They reached the railroad station at 5:30 in the morning, where a special

A 1904 poster featuring the slogan "Stand Pat!" urges voters to stay with Roosevelt for another term. It highlights the Republican campaign themes of sound money, expansion, protection, and prosperity.

train was waiting to rush him to Buffalo. McKinley had died, and Roosevelt took the oath of office in the home of a friend.

From what he called the presidency's "bully pulpit," Roosevelt gave speeches aimed at raising public consciousness about the nation's role in world politics, the need to control the trusts that dominated the economy, the regulation of railroads, and the impact of political corruption. He appointed young, college-educated men to administrative positions. But active as he was, he was cautious in his approach to domestic affairs. Roosevelt recognized that he had become president by accident, and he wanted above all to be elected in his own right. He succeeded in 1904, winning the presidency by a triumphant majority. His vice president was Charles W. Fairbanks.

Domestic Affairs

Roosevelt called his domestic program the Square Deal. He asked for: (1) an attack on the "serious social problems" facing the nation; (2) legislation to allow the regulation of big business; (3) broader control of the railroads; and (4) conservation of natural resources.

Coal Strike of 1902

Members of the United Mine Workers union in May 1902 went on strike in the anthracite fields of Pennsylvania to obtain a shorter working day, better wages, and union recognition. The mine owners stubbornly refused to deal with the unions. As winter approached, Roosevelt threatened to call out troops to operate the mines in the interest of the public. He also brought such pressure upon the owners that, unwillingly, they agreed to arbitrate. The president appointed a special commission of seven. The verdict of these men gave the miners a nine-hour day and a 10 percent wage increase but not recognition of their union as a bargaining agency. Both sides accepted the verdict.

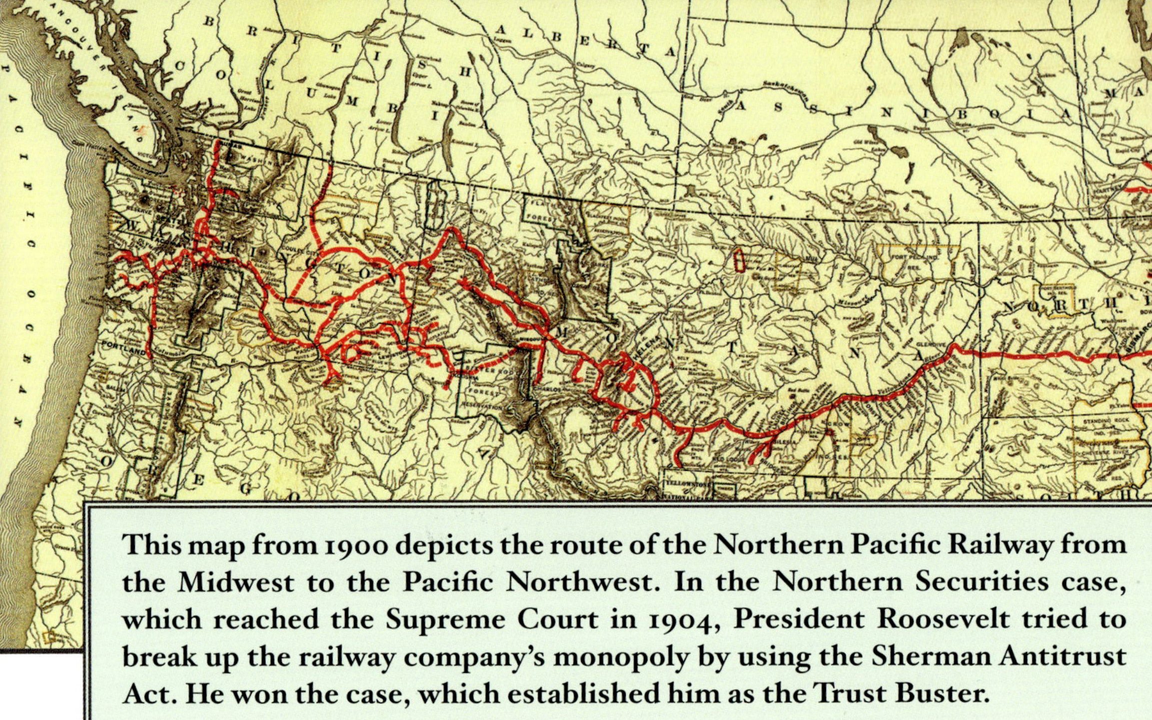

This map from 1900 depicts the route of the Northern Pacific Railway from the Midwest to the Pacific Northwest. In the Northern Securities case, which reached the Supreme Court in 1904, President Roosevelt tried to break up the railway company's monopoly by using the Sherman Antitrust Act. He won the case, which established him as the Trust Buster.

The Trust Buster

Industrial monopolies, popularly known as trusts, were a cause of popular alarm. Roosevelt was not concerned with breaking up the monopolies so much as with correcting their evils. To this end he asked Congress in 1903 to create a Department of Commerce and Labor and a Bureau of Corporations. They were authorized to investigate business combinations and to warn them against practices harmful to the public.

Railroad mergers had produced huge monopolies. About 1901 the Northern Pacific, the Great Northern, and the Burlington systems

were brought together under the Northern Securities Company. In 1903, through Attorney General Philander C. Knox, Roosevelt brought suit under the Sherman Antitrust Act of 1890 for the dissolution of the Northern Securities Company as a conspiracy in restraint of trade. The United States won the suit. Roosevelt continued his policy of "trust-busting" by beginning suits against the United States Steel Corporation, the Standard Oil Company, and other large combinations. In all, Roosevelt obtained twenty-five indictments during his two administrations, although some of the cases were not decided until he was out of office.

In addition to dissolving the Northern Securities Company, Roosevelt attacked railroad monopolies in two acts passed by Congress. The Elkins Act made illegal the granting or accepting of secret rebates; that is, repayments of shipping charges. The Hepburn Act gave the Interstate Commerce Commission the right to fix rates. It extended

The "Muckrakers"

Upton Sinclair, seen here, and Roosevelt exchanged letters in March 1906 about meatpacking practices and the president's plan to have federal inspectors see the conditions at meatpacking houses firsthand.

Public revolt against social evils was further inflamed by a group of writers who, between 1902 and 1908, exposed the evils of business monopoly and government corruption. Best known was Ida M. Tarbell, whose *History of the Standard Oil Company* appeared in *McClure's Magazine* during 1902–03. Lincoln Steffens's *The Shame of the Cities* dealt with corruption in city governments. Upton Sinclair's *The Jungle* described conditions in the meatpacking industry. Sinclair's book was largely responsible for passage of the Federal Food and Drugs Act of 1906.

Such carefully documented works were followed by a flood of irresponsible exposés designed to appeal only to public taste for scandal with little regard for facts. President Roosevelt referred to such writers as "muckrakers." He took the word from a passage in John Bunyan's *Pilgrim's Progress* describing, "the man with the muckrake, the man who could look no way but downward with the muckrake in his hand."

the commission's jurisdiction to include pipelines, terminals, ferries, and express companies. It forbade railroads to grant free passes to anyone but employees, and it forbade the roads to carry commodities in the production of which they were interested.

THE CONSERVATION MOVEMENT

The Far West always held great interest for President Roosevelt. There he had passed happy years on his Elkhorn Ranch in North Dakota, and there he had often hunted big game. The conservation of its great forests and its wildlife was one of his chief concerns. Acting under a Forest Reserve Act of 1891, he withdrew 150 million acres (60,702,846 hectares) of timberland from sale, in addition to 85 million acres (34,398,280 hectares) in Alaska. This land was set aside as national forests under the able administration of Gifford Pinchot, head of the United States Forest Service.

In 1908 Roosevelt called to the White House a conference on the conservation of natural resources. He invited governors, university presidents, businessmen, and scientists to consider what policy ought to be adopted to preserve the nation's resources for the future. As a result of this conference, forty-one states created conservation commissions and a National Conservation Commission was created.

The National Reclamation Act of 1902 authorized the use for irrigation purposes of money obtained from the sale of land in sixteen semiarid states. Under this law dams were built and the task of reclaiming the area was started.

President Roosevelt and naturalist John Muir are seen here at Glacier Point during their three-night camping trip in Yosemite National Park in 1903. Roosevelt and Muir agreed that the country's forests and natural resources needed to be protected.

Foreign Policy

In foreign affairs Roosevelt said his policy was to "speak softly and carry a big stick." He meant that the United States should deal fairly with other countries but also be ready to protect its interests.

The Roosevelt Corollary

Several times during Roosevelt's first years in office, European powers threatened to intervene in Latin America. In January 1903, for example, Great Britain, Germany, and Italy declared a blockade of the ports of Venezuela for the purpose of collecting debts. They proposed to seize the customhouses and pay themselves out of the taxes as they collected them. Roosevelt brought pressure upon the countries involved to arbitrate the claims before the Court of Arbitration at The Hague, and a peaceful settlement was reached.

Roosevelt protested that such threats by European countries were violations of the Monroe Doctrine, which President James Monroe had introduced in 1823. This policy stated that the United States would not permit any European country to interfere in events on the two American continents. To meet the new threats, Roosevelt framed a policy statement in 1904 that became known as the Roosevelt Corollary to the Monroe Doctrine. It stated that the United States would not only bar outside intervention in Latin American affairs but would also police the area and guarantee that countries there met their international obligations.

Roosevelt acted on the policy in 1905, when foreign creditors threatened to intervene in the affairs of the Dominican Republic. Apparently at Roosevelt's suggestion, the president of the Dominican Republic asked the United States to take charge of the collection of customs. An American financial expert remained in charge of the treasury until the debts were paid.

The Panama Canal

Roosevelt resorted to big-stick diplomacy most famously in 1903, when he helped Panama to secede from Colombia. The Hay-Pauncefote Treaty, signed by Britain and the United States in 1901, had cleared the way for an American canal across the Isthmus of

The Big Stick Policy

A political cartoon from 1904 depicts President Roosevelt patrolling the Caribbean with a big stick.

The name that Roosevelt gave his foreign policy came from a West African proverb: "Speak softly and carry a big stick; you will go far." He cited his fondness for the proverb in a letter to a friend while he was still the governor of New York. His first noted public use of the phrase occurred when he championed before Congress increasing naval preparation to support the country's diplomatic goals. The phrase was also used later by Roosevelt to explain his relations with domestic political leaders and his approach to such issues as the regulation of monopolies and the demands of trade unions. The phrase came to be automatically associated with Roosevelt and was frequently used by the press, especially in cartoons, to refer particularly to his foreign policy.

This map of central Panama from around 1900 shows the proposed route of the Panama Canal through the isthmus, which was then part of Colombia. Upon its completion in 1914, the canal connected the Atlantic and Pacific oceans.

Panama. It was followed in 1903 by a treaty with Colombia granting the right to build the canal. The Colombian Senate rejected the treaty. Especially alarmed by Colombia's action were members of the French Panama Canal Company, who would lose $40 million if they did not sell their rights to the United States before their franchise expired in 1904. Using a revolutionist, Philippe Bunau-Varilla, as their agent, they planned a rebellion to free the state of Panama from Colombia.

Roosevelt ordered US naval vessels to keep any hostile forces off the isthmus and to prevent the Colombian troops at Colón

In 1906 President Roosevelt visited Panama to check on the construction of the Panama Canal. The photo shows him operating a steam shovel. Roosevelt considered the construction of the canal his greatest accomplishment as president.

from proceeding to Panama City. The president's explanation was that he wanted to avoid bloodshed and that the United States was bound by treaty to keep the isthmian railroad open. Secretary of State John Hay formally recognized the Republic of Panama, and a few days later the new republic gave the United States control of a 10-mile-wide (16-km-wide) strip across the isthmus.

Construction began at once on the Panama Canal, which Roosevelt visited in 1906, the first president to leave the country while in office. He considered the construction of the canal, a symbol of the triumph of American determination and technological know-how, his greatest accomplishment as president. As he later boasted in his autobiography, "I took the Isthmus, started the canal and then left Congress not to debate the canal, but to debate me."

Alaska Boundary Dispute

Another example of wielding the big stick came when Roosevelt put pressure on Canada in a boundary dispute in Alaska. The eastern boundary of the "panhandle" had been in question since 1825 when Russia concluded

This map shows the Alaska boundary dispute between the United States and Canada. The blue line shows the US border claim, the red line Canada and Britain's claim, and the green line British Columbia's claim; the yellow line marks the modern boundary. A joint arbitration commission of three Americans, two Canadians, and one Briton met in 1903 and upheld the US claim by a vote of four to two.

a treaty with England. Roosevelt let it be known that he was willing to submit to arbitration before a special court of six members, three to be appointed by him and three by the British government. The commission met in London in 1903. The United States was given a strip of coastline along the west border of British Columbia. The award was accepted by both governments and the dispute was thus settled peaceably.

ROOSEVELT AND WORLD POLITICS

Roosevelt showed the soft-spoken, sophisticated side of his diplomacy in dealing with major powers outside the Western Hemisphere. In Asia he was alarmed by Russian expansionism and by rising Japanese power. In September 1905 Roosevelt brought about a peace conference between Russia and Japan, which were then at war. He served as mediator at the conference, which was held in Portsmouth, New Hampshire. More than just to bring peace, Roosevelt wanted to construct a balance of power in Asia that might uphold US interests. For this service Roosevelt was awarded the Nobel Peace Prize.

In 1907 Roosevelt defused a diplomatic quarrel caused by anti-Japanese sentiment in California by arranging the so-called Gentlemen's Agreement, which restricted Japanese immigration. In another informal executive agreement, he traded Japan's acceptance of the American position in the Philippines for recognition by the United States of the Japanese conquest of Korea and expansionism in China. Contrary to his bold public stance, Roosevelt privately came to

President Roosevelt (*center*) poses with peace envoys from Russia and Japan at the signing of the Treaty of Portsmouth in 1905. For his efforts to end the Russo-Japanese War, Roosevelt was awarded the Nobel Peace Prize.

Gentlemen's Agreement

Roosevelt negotiated the Gentlemen's Agreement of 1907 in response to the concerns of Californians who feared that Japanese immigrants (a thousand arrivals monthly) would depress wages and gain control of most of the good farming land. Japan agreed not to issue passports to emigrants to the United States, except to certain categories of business and professional men. In return, Roosevelt agreed to urge the city of San Francisco to reverse an order by which children of Japanese parents were segregated from white students in the schools. The Japanese government carried out faithfully its part of the agreement and the San Francisco school board repealed the segregation order, but the bias and discrimination against Japanese in California continued.

favor withdrawal from the Philippines, judging it to be militarily indefensible, and he gave up any hopes of exerting major power in Asia.

During his second term Roosevelt increasingly feared a general European war. He saw British and US interests as nearly identical, and he was strongly inclined to support Britain behind the scenes in diplomatic controversies. In 1906 France, backed by Britain, and Germany were ready to fight over their interests in Morocco. Roosevelt took the lead in arranging a conference of the powers in Algeciras, Spain. In secret instructions to the US envoys to the conference, Roosevelt told them to maintain formal American noninvolvement in European affairs but to do nothing that would endanger relations between France and Britain. Roosevelt believed the maintenance of Franco-British relations was in the best interests of the United States. Despite his bow toward noninvolvement, Roosevelt had broken with the traditional position of isolation from affairs outside the Western Hemisphere. At Algeciras, US representatives had attended a strictly European diplomatic conference, and their actions favored Britain and France over Germany.

Roosevelt was active in planning the Second Hague Peace Conference, where representatives from forty-four countries adopted rules governing arbitration. One dispute settled by the Permanent Court of Arbitration concerned the rights of American fishermen in Canadian waters (1910). The controversy was settled in favor of the United States.

When Secretary of State John Hay died in 1905 he was succeeded by Elihu Root, who had been the secretary of war. Root in 1908 negotiated the Root-Takahira agreement, in which the United States and Japan agreed to respect each other's territorial possessions in the Pacific and to support Chinese independence and the "open-door policy."

American prestige was further helped by strengthening the army and navy. Roosevelt pushed Congress hard to get an appropriation for two new battleships a year, and he kept the fleet highly efficient. This was shown by the cruise around the world of sixteen battleships, all built since the Spanish-American War. Roosevelt decided on this cruise in 1907 at a moment when relations between Japan and the United States were strained because of anti-Japanese agitation in California and in Congress. He always regarded it as one of his most important contributions to world peace.

Last Years as President

The end of Roosevelt's presidency was stormy. From his bully pulpit, he crusaded against "race suicide," prompted by his alarm at falling birth rates among white Americans, and he tried to get the country to adopt a simplified system of spelling. Especially after a financial panic in 1907, his already strained relations with Republican conservatives in Congress degenerated into a spiteful stalemate that blocked any further domestic reforms.

Roosevelt also moved hastily to punish a regiment of some 160 African American soldiers, some of whom had allegedly engaged in a riot in Brownsville, Texas, in which a man was shot and killed. Although no one was ever indicted and a trial was never held, Roosevelt assumed all were guilty and issued a dishonorable discharge to every member of the group, depriving them of all benefits. Many of the soldiers were close to retirement and several held the Medal of Honor. When Congress condemned his actions Roosevelt replied, "The only reason I didn't have them hung was because I could not find out which ones ... did the shooting." This incident, along with his reliance on executive action to bypass Congress, is why some historians see in Roosevelt's presidency the seeds of abuse that flowered in the administrations of later twentieth-century presidents.

CHAPTER 4

Life After the Presidency

Roosevelt declined to consider a third term and secured the Republican nomination for his friend William H. Taft. He was only fifty years old when he left the White House in March 1909. He was still young and energetic, with wide interests, ample income, and the prospect of many years of active life. He knew he had reached the climax of his career too young. Nothing again could be as exciting as having been president.

The Bull Moose Party

Nevertheless, Roosevelt could not avoid being drawn back into politics. He believed that Taft had failed to carry on his policies

William Howard Taft was Roosevelt's friend and his choice for the Republican presidential nomination of 1908. Taft succeeded Roosevelt in the White House by defeating the Democrat William Jennings Bryan.

and that he was needed to preserve the progressive movement that he had helped to start. His friends urged him to be a candidate for president in 1912. He was beaten for the Republican nomination by Taft under circumstances that led to charges of fraud and "steamroller" methods.

Roosevelt's followers then organized the Progressive Party. They held another convention and nominated Roosevelt for president and Governor Hiram W. Johnson of California for vice president. The party was nicknamed Bull Moose because Roosevelt, when asked how he felt, once replied that he was "fit as a bull moose."

In the presidential campaign Roosevelt promoted a "New Nationalism" that would inspire greater government intervention to promote social justice and the economic welfare of the underprivileged. The campaign was bitter, and Roosevelt's attacks on the "stand pat" Republicans were more venomous than those on the Democrats. He led a gallant fight and made a two months' speaking tour of the country. In Milwaukee, Wisconsin, at the height of the campaign, he was slightly wounded by a man who shot at him. He made his speech that night with the

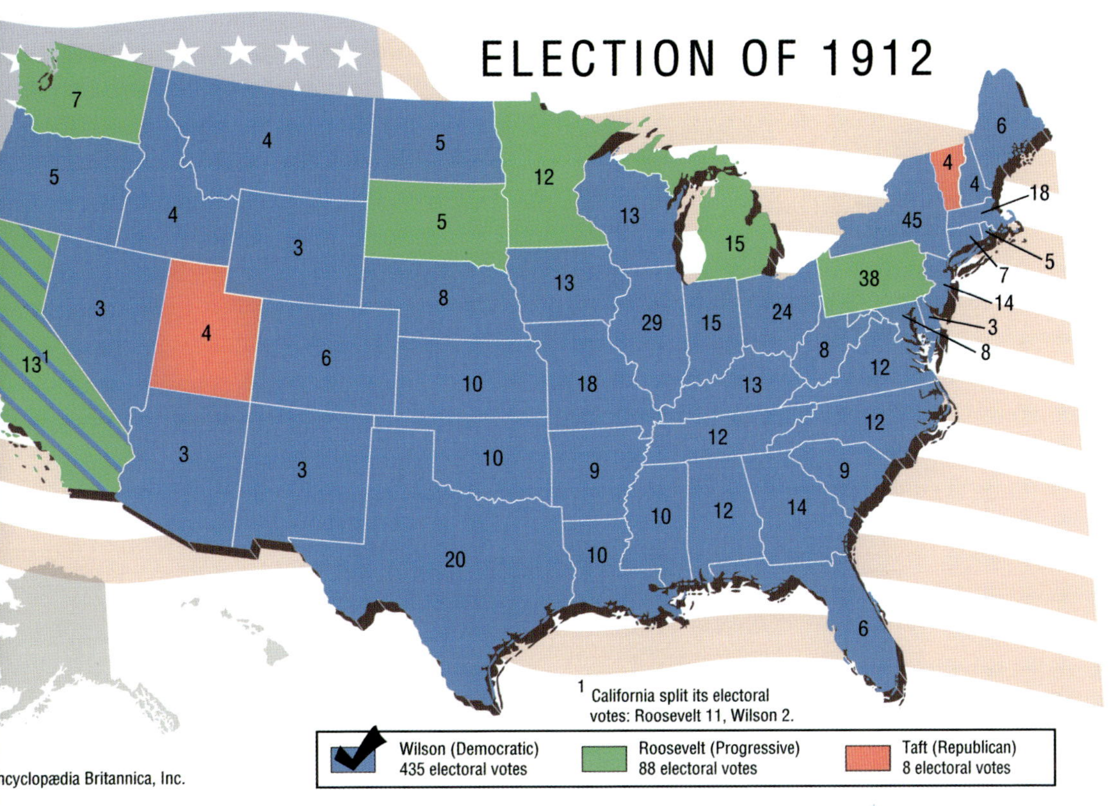

This map shows the results of the US presidential election of 1912. Roosevelt ran for the Progressive, or Bull Moose, Party. Both he and President Taft lost to the Democrat Woodrow Wilson.

bullet lodged in his chest and did not go to the hospital until the meeting had ended. Both Roosevelt and Taft were soundly defeated by the Democrat Woodrow Wilson, who won an impressive 435 electoral votes.

Roosevelt's Travels

Immediately upon leaving office in 1909, Roosevelt left for a ten-month hunting trip in Africa. In March 1910 his wife met him at Khartoum, Sudan, and together they made a tour of Europe. They were entertained by all the royalty of Europe. In Germany, Roosevelt reviewed the troops with Kaiser William. On his return to Sagamore Hill, he wrote another book, *African Game Trails* (1910).

In October 1913 Roosevelt embarked on an expedition into the jungles of Brazil with Brazilian explorer Colonel Cândido Rondon. Roosevelt's son Kermit also joined the expedition. The group surveyed a tributary of the Madeira River called the Rio da Duvida, or River of Doubt, to map it and to collect animal specimens for scientific study. The River of Doubt is a stream filled with rapids and whirlpools. Roosevelt injured his leg on a rock when his canoe overturned. An abscess developed, and he also contracted malaria. The experience brought him near death, but he recovered and returned to New York in May 1914.

No other expedition into the Amazon rainforest was able to explore the River of Doubt successfully until 1926. The Brazilian government later renamed the river as Rio Roosevelt, or Roosevelt River. Roosevelt related his adventures from the expedition in his book *Through the Brazilian Wilderness* (1914).

Roosevelt stands behind a rhinoceros during his African safari and scientific expedition of 1909–1910. After his presidency, Roosevelt traveled to Africa and South America to hunt and to collect specimens for scientific study.

FINAL YEARS

When World War I began in 1914, Roosevelt followed it with keen interest. He soon decided that Wilson "had no policy whatever" and said so in a letter to the author Rudyard Kipling. Roosevelt led rallies for "preparedness," urging Congress to complete the arming of the country. He denounced pacifism. He refused the Progressive Party nomination for president in 1916 and supported Charles Evans Hughes, the Republican nominee. Wilson was reelected.

When the United States declared war against Germany in 1917, Roosevelt hurried to Washington to offer his services. For nearly a year he had been ready with a skeleton organization of a division and with acceptances from the higher officers. To his disappointment and resentment Wilson refused to use Roosevelt's volunteer division. Although he could not go to war, his four sons were all in active service.

By 1918 Roosevelt's support of the war and his harsh attacks on Wilson reconciled Republican conservatives to him, and he was the odds-on favorite for the 1920 nomination. But he died in his sleep on January 6, 1919, less than three months after his sixtieth birthday. He was buried near Sagamore Hill.

Conclusion

When Roosevelt took office in September 1901, he was six weeks short of his forty-third birthday, making him the youngest person ever to enter the presidency. He transformed the public image of the office at once. He renamed the executive mansion the White House and threw open its doors to entertain cowboys, prizefighters, explorers, writers, and artists. His refusal to shoot a bear cub on a 1902 hunting trip inspired a toy maker to name a stuffed bear after him, and the teddy bear fad soon swept the country. His young children romped on the White House lawn, and the marriage of his daughter Alice in 1905 became the biggest social event of the decade.

Roosevelt also made his mark with bold policies, both at home and abroad. He expanded the powers of the presidency and of the federal government and steered the nation toward an active role in world politics. He often acted assertively in foreign affairs, even if he did not have the support of Congress. With the Roosevelt Corollary to the Monroe Doctrine, he asserted that the United States would act as a police power in cases of flagrant and chronic wrongdoing by a Latin American country. He deepened US involvement in Latin America by securing the route for and beginning construction of the Panama Canal.

Wildflowers bloom in the badlands of Theodore Roosevelt National Park in western North Dakota. Roosevelt first went to the area in 1883 to hunt bison.

At home, Roosevelt's boldest actions came in the area of natural resources. At his urging, Congress created the Forest Service to manage government-owned forest reserves. Simultaneously, Roosevelt exercised existing presidential authority to designate public lands as national forests to make them off-limits to commercial exploitation of lumber, minerals, and waterpower. Roosevelt set aside almost five times as much land as all of his predecessors combined, 194 million acres (78.5 million hectares). In commemoration of Roosevelt's dedication to conservation, Theodore Roosevelt National Memorial Park in North Dakota, which includes his Elkhorn Ranch, and Theodore Roosevelt Island in Washington, DC, a 91-acre (37-hectare) wooded island in the Potomac River, were named in his honor.

Roosevelt's home in Oyster Bay, Long Island, and his boyhood home in New York City were established as national historic sites in 1962 and 1965, respectively. Although Roosevelt had been nominated in 1916 to receive a US Army Medal of Honor for his heroism during the Battle of Santiago, he was not awarded the medal until President Bill Clinton posthumously bestowed it in 2001. Roosevelt is the only president to have received the honor.

Glossary

abscess A painful area of inflamed tissue that is filled with pus.

administrative Of or relating to administration, or the management of public affairs as distinguished from policy-making.

agitation The attempt or act of stirring up public feeling or influencing public opinion.

arbitrate To settle a disagreement after hearing the arguments of both sides.

asthma A respiratory disorder that is marked by difficulty in breathing with wheezing, a feeling of tightness in the chest, and coughing.

chronic Continuing or occurring again and again for a long time.

corollary Something added to a speech or document.

cowpuncher Cowboy.

dissolve To bring to an end; terminate.
flagrant Too bad to overlook.
forensics The art or study of debate.
franchise A special privilege granted to an individual or group; especially, the right to be and exercise the powers of a corporation.
inauguration A ceremonial induction into office.
malaria A serious disease that causes chills and fever and that is passed from one person to another by the bite of mosquitoes.
Medal of Honor A US military decoration awarded in the name of the Congress for exceptional bravery in battle.
monopoly Complete control over the entire supply of goods or a service in a certain market.
muckraker One of a group of writers noted for exposing abuses and misconduct in American business, government, and society in the early twentieth century.
nearsighted Able to see near things more clearly than distant ones.
strenuous Showing or requiring great energy and effort.
trust A combination of firms or corporations formed by a legal agreement.

For More Information

American Historical Association (AHA)
400 A Street SE
Washington, DC 20003
(202) 544-2422
Website: http://www.historians.org
A professional organization, the AHA promotes the study of history and teaching history as a career. It awards fellowships and grants and provides access to important resources and publications in the field of history.

American Museum of Natural History (AMNH)
Central Park West at 79th Street
New York, NY 10024-5192
(212) 769-5100
Website: http://www.amnh.org
The AMNH features a permanent exhibit

about Theodore Roosevelt's lifelong commitment to the natural world in its Theodore Roosevelt Memorial Hall.

Miller Center
PO Box 400406
Charlottesville, VA 22904
(434) 924-7236
Website: http://millercenter.org/president/roosevelt
Part of the University of Virginia, the Miller Center focuses on the study of presidents, their policies, and political history. The website's Theodore Roosevelt page provides essays on his life and presidency, information on the First Lady and members of Roosevelt's administration, and an image gallery.

Sagamore Hill National Historic Site
20 Sagamore Hill Road
Oyster Bay, NY 11771
(516) 922-4788
Website: http://www.nps.gov/sahi
Also known as the Summer White House, Sagamore Hill was the home of Theodore Roosevelt and his family from 1885 until Roosevelt's death in 1919.

Theodore Roosevelt Birthplace National Historic Site
28 East 20th Street
New York, NY 10003
(212) 260-1616
Website: http://www.nps.gov/thrb
Theodore Roosevelt was born at 28 East Twentieth Street in New York City. The house that stands at the location today is a reconstruction of the original and contains about half of its original furnishings.

Theodore Roosevelt Collection
Houghton Library and Widener Library
Harvard University
c/o Library Privileges Office
Widener Library, Room 130
Harvard Yard
Cambridge, MA 02138
(617) 495-4166
Website: http://hcl.harvard.edu/libraries/houghton/collections/roosevelt.cfm#contact
The Theodore Roosevelt Collection, which is housed in Harvard's Houghton and Widener libraries, is a principal resource for studying Roosevelt's life.

The holdings include correspondence of Roosevelt and his family, diaries, speeches, books, articles, and archives of the Progressive Party.

Theodore Roosevelt Inaugural National Historic Site
641 Delaware Avenue
Buffalo, NY 14202
(716) 884-0095
Website: http://www.nps.gov/thri
This national historic site is the house in which Roosevelt took the oath of office as the twenty-sixth president after the assassination of President William McKinley in 1901. Exhibits and guided tours tell the story of the inauguration.

Theodore Roosevelt National Park
PO Box 7
Medora, ND 58645
(701) 623-4466
Website: https://www.nps.gov/thro/index.htm
Park visitors can learn about Theodore Roosevelt, his ranch, and the period of the western expansion, among other historical and cultural subjects.

The White House
1600 Pennsylvania Avenue NW
Washington, DC 20500
(202) 456-1111
Website: https://www.whitehouse.gov
The White House is the official office and residence of the president of the United States. The White House's website provides information about the history of the building, the First Ladies, and the presidents, including Theodore Roosevelt (https://www.whitehouse.gov/1600/presidents/theodoreroosevelt).

Websites

Because of the changing nature of internet links, Rosen Publishing has developed an online list of websites related to the subject of this book. This site is updated regularly. Please use this link to access the list:

http://www.rosenlinks.com/PPPL/roosevelt

For Further Reading

Baker, Brynn. *Roosevelt's Rough Riders: Fearless Cavalry of the Spanish-American War* (Fact Finders). North Mankato, MN: Capstone Press, 2016.

Berne, Emma Carlson. *The Presidency of Theodore Roosevelt: Leading from the Bully Pulpit* (Greatest U.S. Presidents). North Mankato, MN: Compass Point Books, 2015.

Burgan, Michael, and Jerry Hoare. *Who Was Theodore Roosevelt?* (Who Was—?). New York, NY: Grosset & Dunlap, 2014.

Fitzpatrick, Brad. *Theodore Roosevelt* (Conservation Heroes). New York, NY: Chelsea House Publishers, 2011.

Grayson, Robert, and Nancy Beck Young. *The Roosevelts* (America's Great Political Families). Minneapolis, MN: ABDO Publishing, 2016.

Hajeski, Nancy. *The Big Book of Presidents: From George Washington to Barack Obama*. New York, NY: Skyhorse Publishing, Inc., 2015.

Hamilton, John. *Theodore Roosevelt National Park* (National Parks). Edina, MN: ABDO Publishing Company, 2009.

Henry, Mike. *Tell Me About the Presidents: Lessons for Today's Kids from America's Leaders*. Lanham, MD: Rowman & Littlefield, 2015.

Key, M. David. *Rough Rider: The Life of Theodore Roosevelt*. Annapolis, MD: Naval Institute Press, 2013.

McPherson, Stephanie Sammartino. *Political Parties: From Nominations to Victory Celebrations*. Minneapolis, MN: Lerner Publications, 2016.

Murphy, Frank, and Richard Walz. *Take a Hike, Teddy Roosevelt!* (Step into Reading). New York, NY: Random House, 2015.

Roosevelt, Theodore. *An Autobiography of Theodore Roosevelt.* Stephen Vincent Brennan, ed. New York, NY: Skyhorse Publishing, 2011.

Roosevelt, Theodore. *The Rough Riders*. New York, NY: Fall River Press, 2014.

Schwartz, Heather E. *Theodore Roosevelt's Presidency* (Presidential Powerhouses). Minneapolis, MN: Lerner Publications, 2015.

Vander Hook, Sue. *Building the Panama Canal* (Essential Events). Edina, MN: ABDO Publishing Company, 2010.

Vietze, Andrew. *Becoming Teddy Roosevelt: How a Maine Guide Inspired America's 26th President*. Rockport, ME: Down East Books, 2010.

Index

S

T

U

V

W